For My Father

AMIRA THORON

Pleasure Boat Studio: A Literary Press
New York

For My Father, by Amira Thoron

ISBN 978-0-912887-05-0
Library of Congress Control Number: 2014933015
First U.S. Printing

Design by Susan Ramundo
Cover by Lauren Grosskopf

Pleasure Boat Studio books are available through your favorite bookstore and through **SPD (Small Press Distribution), Partners/West, Baker & Taylor, Ingram, Brodart, Amazon.com,** and **bn.com**

and also through our website via credit card:
PLEASURE BOAT STUDIO: A LITERARY PRESS
www.pleasureboatstudio.com
201 West 89th Street
New York, NY 10024

Contact **Jack Estes**
Fax: 413-677-0085
Email: pleasboat@nyc.rr.com

C.T.
1930–1974

Do you watch for me? Are you there?
Your pocketknife lies rusted shut. A lock of hair
awaits ceremonious burial. A gold St Christopher
medal engraved with unknown initials.
I tied them to me with a square knot.
A bowline. A figure-eight. Cleat.

Bow. Mast. Stern. At nine I memorized the parts
of a boat, hoping to bind you to me with lines
tasting of salt. An anchor. So much I lost
overboard when my small boat capsized. Water
swept away my blue jean shorts; my sunglasses dropped,
their open arms helplessly turning into the green.

I watch home movies where you sail out towards distant islands.
In my mind I hear the snap of the sail, the rush
of water beneath the boat, the creaking mast.
It is your last summer and I want you
to turn around and come home to me.
I comb the beach for signs you washed ashore.

One day a letter arrives, your voice from the sea,
  I am alone on the darkened water—
A sonnet you wrote from your navy ship.
For fifty years it lay, hidden between brittle pages:
a scrapbook, the images sepia and fading.
I did not know how closely we were tied, you and I.

Did I pluck my images from your skin? Is it your moon
I write about, your voice that pours through my tongue,
that seeps into my skin like soil following the seam in a stone?
On its lichened surface I danced; skinned knees, mosquito bitten legs.
Waving my orange popsicle in the air I declared a holiday of wings.
Were you there in the branches above my head?

Were your eyes the deformed bulges in the bark?
Do you remember the rope swing? How we cousins
shouted and sang? I remember. Though mostly I was alone,
a barefoot child following the mossy path,
careful to watch translucent Indian pipes
rise from shattered brown leaves.

For My Father

I have returned home,
my stomach full of leaves—

One

Water seeks its own level;
there is a leak I cannot find.
All summer long I watch a horizontal crack
crawl along the bathroom wall,
the light blue paint bubble and pock.
I dream of this house again and again;
dreams of structure, frame, and lintel.
Once, I formed a sleeping porch.
Once, I formed a door.
What secrets lie in hollows and out buildings beyond the hill?
Moths lie dead between the window and sill.

In Grandmother's bedroom
mildew crawls
across chipped paint,
peeled plaster.
Her horsehair mattress
lies exposed
on bare springs.

•

I loved her violet scent, the cool
smoothness of her palms
when she took my hand
to cross the street.
It was the only touch.

•

Carefully I step between rolled rugs
and sheet draped furniture
to pull out favorite books
whose brittle faded spines
come apart in my hands.

•

I have not set foot here before except
to lay clean laundry on her bed
or pass through to her bathroom where
she dressed an oozing poison ivy wound
or removed a tick from my inner thigh.

Standing at the threshold I still long
for a tenderness she could only express
in the order of things, in the regularity
of meals, in the rows of pressed sheets
stacked in the linen cupboard.

I submitted to both her order and her wisdom:
how to lay a breakfast tray, make a bed, address
an envelope. How to dry dishes, shine silver,
arrange cookies on a plate. How to dress,
how to stand, how to pronounce the words,

the accents, the syllables. She adjusted
the intonation of my voice, the cadence
of my walk, the level of my eyes.
From her I learned the names
of authors, of plants, trees and birds.

Together we observed spiders no smaller
than a pin head swarm from a punctured
egg sac. We noted the flight of a ruby-
throated hummingbird as it darted
from an orange daylily.

I stand at the threshold. I look down,
I look away. I cannot hold my gaze.
Again I am cowed. Again I am captured,
pinned on red velvet, my palms sweating
beside her as she reads out loud to me.

A sea wind brushes past my face; white
curtains rise and billow. I cross the room
to her chest of drawers to find unopened
packages of silver hairnets beside gauzy
pressed handkerchiefs smelling of mildew.

I finger a green tube of red lipstick and a jar
of face powder. I lift a grey mohair shawl
sheer as a spider's web and wrap it around
my shoulders. In the mirror, I catch
my startled face, *Am I a ghost or a thief?*

And in the final drawer, laid carefully in the corner,
a plastic bag filled with all the notes I wrote
and tucked under her pillow: rows and rows
of magic marker drawn hearts, rainbow balloons.
All my love letters until I stopped speaking to her.

•

Today, she tried to kill me with the meat cleaver.
Left me slumped over the sink
with only two more potatoes to peel
and the lamb still roasting in the oven.
She did not like the changes I made
in the dining room. The paintings moved,
the china disturbed, the table hacked to pieces.

Thankfully, I came to when the timer rang.
With little loss of blood (just a nick above my right eye)
I removed the sizzling mass
and placed it on the counter to harden and cool.
I found her in the living room,
the air above her chair seething and thick.

Tonight, as I lie in my childhood room
my horsehair mattress crunches and sags.
I hear her downstairs calling and calling.
I've left the kitchen door open
for the raccoons to have their feast:
their little clawed hands, little sharp teeth
devouring the pink-grey meat.

●

In sleep I hear
her crying teeth
to knees. Spine
rattles against mine.

I cannot reach her.
We know
the viscous breath
of moles, the furtive

diggings of skunk,
grubs coiled
in moonlight.
Night presses.

Behind the wall
tiny jaws
seek succor
from paper, from dust.

●

June 4th, 1945

St. Paul's School
Concord, NH

Dear Mum,

I can only stand a certain number of shocks, what with dogs and Daddies I am not going to live much longer, I am fine. Anniversary was tons of fun, our team won 1, 4, 5 (mine), 6, 7 races.

Tell Daddy I am very glad I took rowing. There is nothing like it and I will always take it. I am very busy these days.

Love—

•

I kneel and pull
onion-scented snowdrop
bulbs from soil
Grandmother sifted
through cool hands
that rarely touched me.
I fill holes
with water and press
seedlings hard to earth.
Here we planted impatiens.
Here we staked platycodon.
This was Grandfather's rose garden.
Forty years later
one peach rose remains.
What did Grandmother do with his roses?
Was it too much work
to wrap them each fall
in burlap and string?
Could she not protect
them from frost,
aphids and rot?
Did she let them die
or did she snip
each branch, each twig
before unearthing roots
with a rusted pitchfork?

•

In the woods
I find remains.
Several yards from the dirt road
ferns protrude: little whiskers growing out of moss.
Mosquitoes swarm and the mound
beneath my feet
heaves and crunches.
A young sassafras has taken root.

Here, layers of the discarded:
broken jam jars and milk bottles,
white enameled chamber pots,
and cans rusted to a dark brown lace.
Are you here, too? Her beloved son?
Forty years your boat lies
raised on saw-horses in the barn.
Mice have gnawed the straps,
the centerboard is gone.

I asked her once to tell me
stories of her boy:
I had opened a picture book
to your child-crooked scrawl.
Rising from her chair,
the glass of bourbon swayed.
No, she hissed, *I will not*.

•

Listen:
the silence is murderous.
It startles my tongue.
I taste metal. I taste wood.
In this house,
sacred to mice and wasps,
I raise the blade.
This time I'm a savage.
This time I wield it
clean above my head
and slam it into wood.
The dining table shudders and splits.
We speak of faith.
We speak of resurrection.
But I remember,
my plump child hands before you
how metal turned to rust.

•

Downstairs I find a box:
condolence letters
with answer dates
written across the corners
in blue ink.

As she finishes each letter,
she places it
along the table's edge
as if to sort a seating plan
or the invitations to a lunch.

For what else is there to do
but apply order
and make lists?
To mark corners with notations,
Letter   Flowers   Donation

January 9, 1974

Dear Violet, dear Ben—

At dusk tonight I went out and walked in the beautiful fresh snow around your house and thought of you and of ———.

What a splendid man he must have been! I hardly knew him directly, having only barely met a couple of times but from all the things said about him I knew he was just great. You must have been very proud to have such a son.

The spirit has its own qualities and its own way of going on. I am sure there is a Peace—but that it is a very active thing. Alfred North Whitehead expressed it well, "Peace is a quality of mind, steady in its reliance that fine action is treasured in the Nature of Things" I deeply believe that and its consequences are tremendous.

•

A host of ghostly white Indian pipes
unfurls out of moss.
Mushrooms red-bulbous and sliding.
My sheets are damp:
the wind a constant ache
in my spine, in my finger joints.
I yearn for easing.

•

Upstairs, the rooms stifle with air so still
I hear the ocean, or is that the wind
in my copper beech tree?
Massive creature, it rises high above the house
with branches that extend far over roots,
over moss, over lichened stone walls.

Its trunk holds pools of rainwater,
pools where I dip my fingers as I climb
the grey-blue branches with their thin-
skinned bark smooth to my bare feet.
From there I can see my bedroom
and her bedroom beside mine.

I can see the tops of the oak trees
and the rooster weather vane
swinging in the wind. Such swaying
in the purple-brown leaves yet where I perch
the woods are still but for the screech
of the red-tail hawk circling the sky above me.

Two

•

Do you remember
the last time?

an apartment
a chair
a blanket

your knees
too fragile
for me

afraid,
we no longer played.
Mother made

Ovaltine

•

Cairo 1973:
sunlight floods
the dining room.

I am in my highchair
pulled to the middle
of a vast dining table.

You, hidden behind your paper,
I see only the top
of your head, your hands.

•

Weekend mornings I pull the blankets
and stuffed animals from my crib
and trot down the short hallway to the foot
of your bed where I sit and wait for you.
One morning you lean over and whisper,
It's too early, come back later.

•

In the car you tear
a stick of Wrigley's
Double-Mint gum in half.

I kneel in my seat
and look backwards
at traffic in the roundabout.

•

In photos you dance
red suit
head tilt
    Your arms
        uplifted

•

The place where I once knew you
derelict,
    obscured.

In a photo
I sleep
on your belly.

In a photo
by the Christmas tree,
I lean into your shoulder
ever so slightly.

As a teenager
I wondered,
Did you ever love me?

•

In your pinstripe suit,
you stand tall by the door.

A green paper wrapper,
a piece of gum torn in half—

you hold it towards me.

What about the boy you played
tennis with the summer before you died?

What did you say to him as he hit
your volleys, your rallies,
your forehands and backhands?

I imagine the freshness of those mornings,
the grass still wet with dew
as you climb the hill to the clay court.

I know how the water tastes from the spigot
by the gate, how you dip your heads
beneath it when you are done.

In the heat of July it is hard to imagine snow.
Soon it will fall without you in this world.

•

The night of your funeral
the house was thick
with the smell of lilies.

It followed Mother
to the bedroom
where she slept.

She woke to find you
seated beside her on the bed.
Stroking her hair you said,
I've come to tuck you in.

•

Items arrive in the mail and mind—
a black and white photograph—
figures fading now, yellowing over time.
Everything wavers so—the tall grasses in the field,
the branches heavy,
purple with choke-berries
thick clustered on the stem.
I find a signature in a guest book,
letters on a desk—*January 5th, 1974.*
Mother writes
your last words to me;
over the phone you said,
Listen, Amira:
I want to say good-bye.
I will not see you again.

•

The red-tailed hawk shrieks,
startled from the field.
A snake curls in his talons.
Rising into the wind,
he never stops shrieking.

I dream of hurricanes.
I fight with absence.
I fling my body
against air and still
you do not rise.

A torn gum wrapper?
A whispered sentence?

Come to me!

Up the dirt road
through silent trees
he climbs.

His wool coat catches
on his sweater and pulls
against his arms.

Unbuttoning it
he wonders,

                Is it cold or stillness

which presses my lungs

                   like sea water?

•

Blood pulses
in my ears
pushes
along
my temples
I cannot
stop
the rush—

•

At five I held
a butcher knife
to my heart.

At seven I climbed
over balconies
eleven stories up.

In my family
we did not
speak of it.
We did not speak.

•

broken Ray Bans
business cards
a pocket knife
a fountain pen

your empty suits hang
in my closet:
black pinstripe
red corduroy

•

In the guest room
I watch Mother dress
for dinner. Little silver
coins on her dress

tinkle as she crosses
the room for her perfume,
as she stands before
the mirror, brushing her hair.

It is a sound from
some other place
I cannot recall. My mind
trips and trips over itself;

the proximity of her body,
the smell of her perfume—
I want to capture them. I want
to capture her, wrap my arms

around her waist, and hold her
and hold her here forever.
From upstairs my nanny calls.
I must dress too.

Later, from my little chair
beside Grandmother,
I watch as she enters
the living room.

Long black hair,
dark eyes lined with kohl,
her colorful dress sways
with the tinkle of beads.

As she steps across
the threshold,
I am suddenly ashamed.
She does not belong here.

●

At boarding school
carved wooden plaques
line the dark
paneled walls
of the dining hall

1915   Grandfather
1948   Father

I run my fingers
along the letters of your name,
the only place where I can touch you—

(there is no grave)

•

Sea water
floods an empty shell

the conch
the moon snail
the periwinkle

I have   no voice
no sound

●

I chose a cord
for my throat,
a tightening
against words
or was it
words
themselves
which coiled
around
my throat
and tugged
until
I would speak?

It is not meant to be this way.
It is not meant to be this way.

•

Under fluorescent lights I sit. 1:30 am. No sleep
despite drugs which make me sweat.
They tried to stop the racing in my head, the
shaking in my body. Voices hurt my skin.

The bearded Yeshiva student argues
with the nurses. Texts from the Torah.
I draw pictures: a copper beech tree,
a stone wall, an osprey in her nest.

I draw a sail far across the Sound
and the cliffs rising behind it.
Yet, the only sea I can imagine
is warm, blood soaked.

He leaves the road

to climb
where water lies
a blue-grey band
        across open sky.

Below him
        our house
        shut up and trim.

I can smell the cleanness
in the air,
feel the

silence of   trees.
He breathes.

Up the dirt road
to our—

•

Listen:
the widows wait
in the living room.

Upstairs,
I am drowning
in glass.

In my family
we do not
speak of it.
We do not speak.

●

Your throat gurgles.
I am covered in blood.
I am glad.

I wanted to smash
every bit of you.
I wanted to watch

your lips turn blue,
your open eyes glaze.
Pressing my cheek

against your wiry curls,
I breathe
the distillation of salt and soap.

Listen,
I whisper as I touch
your mouth,

as I run my hands
over skin stretched tight
against your skull.

Listen,
I want to say good-bye.
I will not see you again.

•

Ferns choke daylilies,
we must have them shorn.
Daylilies grow back
and ferns, they return.

•

Listen:
the whippoorwills are gone.
Even as a child
I rarely heard them.

Whiskered bird,
nest scraped in gravel.
Easy prey for feral cats.
Once I asked,
Do the hunters shoot whippoorwill?

•

Where is the cord
that runs
between this world
and the next?

Buried telephone cables
pulled by fault lines,
by drifting
continental plates.

They held
your hands,
such tiny hairs
flaked skin
thinned
tearing—

•

Your body lies in state,
sealed for public viewing
while behind the wall I wander
and crawl, crawl along a crack
to slither in your ear.
I tunnel the corals
of your brain.
I slink the rivers
of your nervous system,
your brain stem.
I chew and chew
every taught nerve
and edge of you,
chew until I know
something—anything—
for like a cancer,
I infest you.

Through silent trees
          he breathes and strides
to where the road turns
and the woods open
to a pitched field.

There, just beyond
          lies our empty house.

Weathered-grey shingles
windows dark as pond water
          circling—

●

Mornings I run emerald woods
and black-topped roads
through summer green fields.

Will I ever catch a glimpse of you?
A movement between the trees?
A shadow skirting the edge of a field?

I want to know you by touch—

•

diplomat
operative
station chief
cubist communist
philanderer
thief

your silence
gives me nothing

nothing as I patter
and patter away
searching the essence
of you—

•

When you
died
the smell
of Easter lilies
filled
your room,

wound
thick
and sweet
through
the hallway,
past

the nurses' station
into
the elevator,
the grey
stair-
well.

How long
did it drift
under
white
fluorescent
light?

•

Mother and I alone on the train.
Everything is over.
You are gone.
Winter burnt fields
and icy marsh
rush behind us.
She shows me how,
with the tip of her finger
she can spin
her blue scarab ring
on its gold axis.
Leaning into her lap
I try to spin it too
but my three-year-old fingers
are too clumsy.
Over and over
her finger taps
the ancient stone.
I watch and feel
our yearning rise
and press itself
against the wonder
of that spinning stone,
against the blur
of abandoned factories,
the rush and sway
of the derelict,
the unfamiliar,
as our Northbound train
hurtles into dusk.

At dusk the night my father dies
a man steps
over a stone wall
he walks through
            a beetle bung grove
past the skeletal beach plums
down to the snow-
covered lawn where
the copper beech tree rises
massive and silent.

My father has left this earth.
How is it that snow still falls?

●

I kneel in graveyard dust. It's forty years
since Mother brought your ashes here.
You asked to be buried where
each dawn summons the muezzin's call
and voices of school children rise from
the church beyond these walls.

Your headstone is split, your name veiled
in dust. Here, amongst these foreign graves
you are nobody. I live too far away to tend you.
I cannot sweep the layers of sand nor keep
dead leaves from the land your small grave
claims. I cannot bring water to the strange
plants whose spiny leaves cover your name.

I have traveled here twice. The first time,
I was eighteen—I could not even look.
Today, I cannot stop crying. Where are you?
In which place shall I find you?
Here, amongst the graves of an ancient city?
Or high in the branches of my copper beech tree?

Come to me.

O Empty House.
O Night Sky.
Delineate
    the forgotten.

O Glacial Stone
and Light of Snow:
    press into stillness
        I do not yet know.

O Empty House:
I bring you
my copper leaves
    dipped in silver.

O Moon: appear.
    Follow me home.
(Will he?)

Circle
our empty house,
be the only   breath.

I bend
    like water—
for I am not drowning,
I am full
    of leaves.

My throat holds
this chalice
and I—

    Drink.

ACKNOWLEDGMENTS

Versions of "In Sleep I Hear" and "When You" first appeared in *The Tiny*.

I'd like to thank the following for their help and encouragement in the completion of this book: Casey Barrett, Nell Broley, June Cohen, Penelope Cray, Laura Cronk, Deborah D'Arcy, Eric Delson, Jack Estes, Connie Fulenwider, Rita Gabis, Mike Garrett, Shanti Hulsebus, Fanny Howe, Megin Jimenez, Marisol Kaminski, Sarah Leahy, Ruth McCollough, Jill McKeon, Bill MacArthur, Luz Thoron-MacArthur, Alicia Mugetti, Aaron Raymond, Enrique Rodriguez, Laurie Sheck, Victoria Sanford, Jennifer Tseng, and Margot Wilkie.

Special loving thanks to Elise Thoron.

And to my husband, William Edward Harry Harcourt-Smith.

ABOUT THE AUTHOR

Amira Thoron was born in Cairo, Egypt and raised in New York City and Martha's Vineyard, Massachusetts, where she spent summers with her paternal grandmother. She received her BA in English from Brown University and her MFA in Poetry from The New School. She lives in New York City and Martha's Vineyard. This is her first book.

Poetry Books from *Pleasure Boat Studio: A Literary Press*

Listed chronologically by release date. **Note: Empty Bowl Press** is a Division of Pleasure Boat Studio.

Return to a Place Like Seeing ~ John Palmer ~ $17
Ascendance ~ Tim McNulty ~ $16
Alter Mundus ~ Lucia Gizzino ~ trans. from Italian by Michael Daley ~ $15.95
The Every Day ~ Sarah Plimpton ~ $15.95
A Taste ~ Morty Schiff ~ $15.95
Hanoi Rhapsodies ~ Scott Ezell ~ $10 ~ an empty bowl book
Dark Square ~ Peter Marcus ~ $14.95
Notes from Disappearing Lake ~ Robert Sund ~ $15
Taos Mountain ~ Paintings and poetry ~ Robert Sund ~ $45 (hardback only)
P'u Ming's Oxherding Pictures & Verses ~ trans. from Chinese by Red Pine ~ $15 ~ an empty bowl book
Swimming the Colorado ~ Denise Banker ~ $16 ~ an empty bowl book
A Path to the Sea ~ Liliana Ursu, trans. from Romanian by Adam J. Sorkin and Tess Gallagher ~ $15.95
Songs from a Yahi Bow: Poems about Ishi ~ Yusef Komanyakaa, Mike O'Connor, Scott Ezell ~ $13.95
Beautiful Passing Lives ~ Edward Harkness ~ $15
Immortality ~ Mike O'Connor ~ $16
Painting Brooklyn ~ Paintings by Nina Talbot, Poetry by Esther Cohen ~ $20
Ghost Farm ~ Pamela Stewart ~ $13
Unknown Places ~ Peter Kantor, trans. from Hungarian by Michael Blumenthal ~ $14
Moonlight in the Redemptive Forest ~ Michael Daley ~ includes a CD ~ $16
Lessons Learned ~ Finn Wilcox ~ $10 ~ an empty bowl book
Jew's Harp ~ Walter Hess ~ $14
The Light on Our Faces ~ Lee Whitman-Raymond ~ $13
Petroglyph Americana ~ Scott Ezell ~ $15 ~ an empty bowl book
God Is a Tree, and Other Middle-Age Prayers ~ Esther Cohen ~ $10
Home & Away: The Old Town Poems ~ Kevin Miller ~ $15
Old Tale Road ~ Andrew Schelling ~ $15 ~ an empty bowl book
Working the Woods, Working the Sea ~ Eds. Finn Wilcox, Jerry Gorsline ~ $22 ~ an empty bowl book
The Blossoms Are Ghosts at the Wedding ~ Tom Jay ~ with essays ~ $15 ~ an empty bowl book
Against Romance ~ Michael Blumenthal ~ $14
Days We Would Rather Know ~ Michael Blumenthal ~ $14
Craving Water ~ Mary Lou Sanelli ~ $15
When the Tiger Weeps ~ Mike O'Connor ~ with prose ~ 15
Concentricity ~ Sheila E. Murphy ~ $13.95
The Immigrant's Table ~ Mary Lou Sanelli ~ with recipes ~ $14
Women in the Garden ~ Mary Lou Sanelli ~ $14
Saying the Necessary ~ Edward Harkness ~ $14
Nature Lovers ~ Charles Potts ~ $10
The Politics of My Heart ~ William Slaughter ~ $13
The Rape Poems ~ Frances Driscoll ~ $13

Desire ~ Jody Aliesan ~ $14 ~ an empty bowl book
Dreams of the Hand ~ Susan Goldwitz ~ $14 ~ an empty bowl book
The Basin: Poems from a Chinese Province ~ Mike O'Connor ~ $10/$20 ~ an empty bowl book (paper/hardbound)
The Straits ~ Michael Daley ~ $10 ~ an empty bowl book
In Our Hearts and Minds: The Northwest and Central America ~ Ed. Michael Daley ~ $12 ~ with prose ~ an empty bowl book
The Rainshadow ~ Mike O'Connor ~ $16 ~ an empty bowl book
Untold Stories ~ William Slaughter ~ $10/$20 ~ an empty bowl book (paper/hardbound)

Our Chapbook Series:

No. 1: *The Handful of Seeds: Three and a Half Essays* ~ Andrew Schelling ~ $7 ~ nonfiction
No. 2: *Original Sin* ~ Michael Daley ~ $8
No. 3: *Too Small to Hold You* ~ Kate Reavey ~ $8
No. 4: *The Light on Our Faces*—re-issued in non-chapbook (see above list)
No. 5: **Eye** ~ William Bridges ~ $8
No. 6: *Selected* **New Poems** *of Rainer Maria Rilke* ~ trans. fm German by Alice Derry ~ $10
No. 7: *Through High Still Air: A Season at Sourdough Mountain* ~ Tim McNulty ~ $9 ~ with prose
No. 8: *Sight Progress* ~ Zhang Er, trans. fm Chinese by Rachel Levitsky ~ $9 ~ prosepoems
No. 9: *The Perfect Hour* ~ Blas Falconer ~ $9
No. 10: *Fervor* ~ Zaedryn Meade ~ $10
No. 11: *Some Ducks* ~ Tim McNulty ~ $10
No. 12: *Late August* ~ Barbara Brackney ~ $10
No. 13: *The Right to Live Poetically* ~ Emily Haines ~ $9

From other publishers (in limited editions):

In Blue Mountain Dusk ~ Tim McNulty ~ $12.95 ~ a Broken Moon Press book
China Basin ~ Clemens Starck ~ $13.95 ~ a Story Line Press book
Journeyman's Wages ~ Clemens Starck ~ $10.95 ~ a Story Line Press book

Orders: Pleasure Boat Studio books are available by order from your bookstore, directly from our website, or through the following:

SPD (Small Press Distribution) Tel. 800-869-7553, Fax 510-524-0852
Partners/West Tel. 425-227-8486, Fax 425-204-2448
Baker & Taylor Tel. 800-775-1100, Fax 800-775-7480
Ingram Tel. 615-793-5000, Fax 615-287-5429
Amazon.com or **Barnesandnoble.com**

Pleasure Boat Studio: A Literary Press
201 West 89th Street
New York, NY 10024
Fax: 413-677-0085
www.pleasureboatstudio.com / pleasboat@nyc.rr.com